MOTIVATION FOR ACTORS

PSYCHOLOGY FOR ACTORS SERIES

ALEXA ISPAS

WORD
BOTHY

CONTENTS

INTRODUCTION

Building a successful acting career takes years of hard graft.

You must be able to handle many rejections and much criticism before you get any chance of getting noticed in the industry.

You must also juggle various bill-paying jobs to keep a roof over your head and be prepared to receive little outside validation for all your efforts.

Finding acting work is hard, and when you do, the parts you are likely to get in the beginning may not be as creatively challenging or exciting as you would like.

All these factors are likely to take a toll on your motivation.

At various times, you will probably feel burned

out, lacking in purpose, and regretting your decision to go into acting.

After a while, you may wonder if you have what it takes to make it in the industry, or whether it is time to quit.

Fortunately, over the past few decades, psychological research has made significant progress in uncovering the principles behind human motivation.

One of the key findings from this research is that, under the right circumstances, motivation grows, leading to unstoppable and energizing momentum.

If you suffer from low motivation, these psychological insights will help you set up the right circumstances for your motivation to grow.

Increasing your motivation will boost your acting career in many ways.

More motivation will energize you to continuously develop your acting skills, which will lead to more auditions and opportunities coming your way.

You will be better prepared in auditions and rehearsals, and initiate your own projects, so you do not rely exclusively on outside work.

You will also find it easier to complete boring

yet necessary career-related tasks, such as putting together a list of potential agents or editing your showreel.

Motivation is also essential in keeping up your energy and enthusiasm through the creatively uninspiring acting jobs you are likely to get at the beginning of your acting career.

If you want to activate your inner drive and take your acting career to the next level, this book will give you all the necessary knowledge and tools.

You will learn how to increase your motivation by creating shifts in your brain chemistry, and how to avoid de-motivating yourself.

You will also learn simple yet powerful tools that provide the ideal circumstances for your motivation to grow.

In the final chapter, we will address the kinds of problems that arise for actors in relation to their motivation, and how to deal with them.

I have kept this book short, so you can read it in an afternoon and gain access to all the tools you need to increase your motivation and build a successful acting career.

CHAPTER 1

MOTIVATION AS AN ACTOR

EXTRINSIC VS. INTRINSIC MOTIVATION

Psychological studies show there are two types of motivation: extrinsic and intrinsic.

Extrinsic motivation depends on external factors, such as praise or punishment; the so-called "carrot and stick approach."

If you fear forgetting your lines during an audition, you will work harder to memorize them.

Intrinsic motivation comcs from within and is driven by your own goals.

Becoming better at memorization may be something you do because you want to develop this valuable skill, not because of any external pressures.

To build a successful acting career, you need a lot of intrinsic motivation.

This is especially the case during the early years, when you are new to the industry and there is no outside validation coming your way.

As an actor, competition is higher than in almost any other profession, and the odds of success are low.

If you simply wait for a great part to fall into your lap, you will get lost among the crowd of hopefuls, no matter how talented you are.

To maximize your chances, you must get into the habit of setting your own goals and making things happen.

DEVELOPING INTRINSIC MOTIVATION

A common misconception is that intrinsic motivation works like a personality trait: you either have it or you don't.

In fact, research on so-called "high achievers"– people who have reached success in their chosen field–shows that intrinsic motivation is not usually something high achievers are born with or display at an early age.

The most motivated individuals were initially more extrinsically than intrinsically motivated.

It was only through following good working habits and seeing the results of their hard work that this largely extrinsic motivation became intrinsic.

As research shows, intrinsic motivation grows over time, and it does so with the help of external factors.

Intrinsic and extrinsic motivation are different, but they are not separate.

Although you need to develop your intrinsic motivation, you can use external motivators to encourage this process to happen.

If the right circumstances are present, or you know how to create the right circumstances, you can *become* intrinsically motivated.

This is worth keeping in mind if you need more motivation.

The better you understand how motivation works, the more skilled you will be at setting up circumstances that allow intrinsic motivation to grow.

BRAIN CHEMISTRY AND MOTIVATION

Your intrinsic motivation can go up or down, depending on changes in your brain chemistry.

Even small shifts in brain chemistry lead to noticeable changes in your level of intrinsic motivation.

In turn, your brain chemistry is influenced by the structures that govern your life, such as your habits and time commitments.

The good news is that you can create circumstances that make it easier–and inevitable–to become intrinsically motivated.

By learning to nudge your brain in the right direction, you can gain control over your intrinsic motivation.

Once you know how to set up external factors that increase motivation, you will be on the path to unstoppable and exhilarating momentum.

In addition to gaining the skills to influence your brain chemistry, you also need to avoid de-motivating yourself without realizing it.

Understanding what not to do will make it easier to recognize when you are in danger of losing your motivation.

You will then be able to make adjustments and regain your sense of momentum.

In the next chapter, we will explore one of the biggest mistakes actors make when trying to build momentum.

KEY POINTS

- Research shows there are two types of motivation: extrinsic motivation, which depends on external factors, and intrinsic motivation, which is driven by your own goals.
- To build a successful acting career, you need lots of intrinsic motivation. This will allow you to keep going in the absence of outside validation and despite many challenges.
- Your intrinsic motivation can go up or down, depending on changes in your brain chemistry.
- You can use external factors to change your brain chemistry in a way that increases your intrinsic motivation, leading to an exhilarating sense of momentum.

CHAPTER 2

THE WILLPOWER FALLACY

WILLPOWER AS A LIMITED RESOURCE

In this chapter, we will discuss how actors unknowingly demotivate themselves by relying too much on their willpower when trying to build momentum.

You may think that actors who are making headway in the industry are doing so because they have a vast reservoir of willpower; this is not necessarily true.

Willpower most likely plays a role in their emerging success, but it is not the sole reason they are making progress.

In fact, if they seem to have an endless supply of energy, you can be sure they are drawing on other resources, besides their willpower, to maintain their momentum.

One problem with relying exclusively on your willpower is that it is a limited resource, as it depends on your energy levels.

You only have a certain amount of willpower available before you need to replenish your energy through rest and relaxation.

Once your willpower runs out, and the short-lived "honeymoon phase" of pursuing a new goal comes to an end, you are likely to feel demotivated and depleted.

At such times, you may resort to procrastination or other unhealthy behaviors, while continuously feeling guilty about not working on your acting career.

Another problem is that when you rely on your willpower, you only have your positive intentions as a guide, with no external framework in place to support these intentions.

To get anything done for your acting career, you therefore have to keep dipping into this limited supply of willpower, as there is nothing else to draw upon.

By contrast, the other areas of your life that require willpower, such as the work you do for your bill-paying job, benefit from the pressures that come from external factors.

Whether you like it or not, you need your bill-paying job to keep a roof over your head, and you probably have a supervisor who ensures you turn up on time and do your work.

Although these external pressures seem restrictive, they ensure that you fulfill your commitments.

If you rely exclusively on your willpower to work on your acting career, and you run out of energy, your acting goals are the first to get neglected.

This is because your acting goals do not have any external framework to support your good intentions, whereas other aspects of your life do.

Even worse, relying exclusively on your willpower and then failing, perhaps multiple times, makes you mistakenly believe you are too "lazy" to succeed.

Feeling bad about yourself is demotivating, which eventually makes it tempting to give up on your acting goals and aspirations.

SETTING UP AN EXTERNAL FRAMEWORK

What people who seem to work tirelessly on their acting career have, perhaps without even realizing, is an external framework that makes it easy to do the right thing.

Setting up this framework does not have to be complicated. The simplest solutions are usually the most effective.

For example, let's say you are trying to lose weight. If you attempt to follow a strict diet and rely on your willpower alone, you will most likely give up after a while.

Alternatively, you could use a small amount of willpower to eliminate all high-fat and high-sugar foods from your house.

By doing so, you would be leveraging an external force–your house being empty of foods you are trying to avoid.

When craving something unhealthy, you would have to put in some effort and go to the shops, making it easier to avoid temptation.

Reaching your acting-related goals is not about how much willpower you have. It is about learning how to use your willpower strategically.

The best use of your willpower is to put an external framework in place which helps you take the right action, and then to maintain this framework when it is in danger of falling apart.

By setting up this external framework, you are making it easier to stick to your acting-related goals without constantly having to dip into your limited supply of willpower.

Willpower is like your car's ignition; you need it to get started.

Once you have taken that initial step, you need the support of external factors–your car's engine, its wheels, and so on–to build the momentum required to get somewhere.

If willpower provides the spark that sets the car into motion, what is the fuel you will use to motivate yourself?

This is where your brain chemistry comes in, which we will explore over the next few chapters.

In the next chapter, we will discuss one big

mistake actors make when using their brain chemistry to increase motivation.

KEY POINTS

- One of the biggest mistakes actors make is relying too much on their willpower to build momentum.
- The problem is that willpower is a limited resource, and as such, it runs out quickly.
- When your willpower runs out, you are likely to resort to procrastination or other unhealthy behaviors, while feeling guilty about not working on your acting career.
- Although willpower is necessary for building a successful career, you must use it strategically.
- The best use of willpower is to set up an external framework that steers your actions in the right direction.

CHAPTER 3

THE COMPETITIVENESS PROBLEM

BRAIN CHEMISTRY AND COMPETITIVENESS

In the previous chapter, we explored how actors often demotivate themselves by relying too much on their willpower–a limited internal resource–instead of harnessing external factors to guide their actions.

In this chapter, we will discuss the other common mistake actors make: motivating themselves by competing with other actors.

Competitiveness is not necessarily bad; it can be a lot of fun.

How many scripts can you read in a month? How many weird-but-interesting auditions did you go to? How many bill-paying jobs have you been fired from because your acting career got in the way?

This type of social competition works like a buddy system. It is a way to have fun with friends, swap stories, and spur each other on to success.

For evolutionary reasons, we are built for competition.

When you compete with others, your brain releases serotonin, a so-called "happy chemical" that improves your mood and well-being.

The way serotonin boosts your mood is by making you feel superior to others.

This is one of our oldest evolutionary mechanisms; it was instrumental to our survival as a species.

Those of our ancestors who strived to be higher ranked than their peers gained access to more food and other resources.

They were therefore better able to survive long enough to pass on their genes.

Our brain has evolved to keep comparing ourselves to others and continuously monitor how we are doing in the social hierarchy.

While there is a certain amount of competitiveness in every career, this type of motivating factor is especially prevalent within the acting industry.

If you already have a competitive streak, life as an actor will bring that out even more.

Good parts–the resources actors fight over, just like our ancestors fought over food–are scarce, and only one actor can get cast in a role.

If you are that person, you will likely feel better about yourself than everyone else who auditioned.

When you experience success by outperforming your peers, the boost in serotonin increases your energy levels.

This feel-good effect motivates you to work harder, which helps you maintain your higher status.

COMPETITIVENESS AND BURNOUT

In the beginning, competitiveness may seem like a great source of motivation.

It is exciting to do better than your peers, working as hard as it takes to maintain your higher status.

However, using competitiveness as your main source of motivation comes with a lot of problems.

Pushing your way to the top makes you unpleasant to be around and can lead to difficulties forming meaningful bonds with your fellow actors.

Continuously focusing your attention on how others are doing and comparing yourself to them damages your sense of belonging.

Although your motivation and work ethic look admirable from the outside, being fueled by competitiveness is not good for you as a human being.

Being competitive also means you lose touch with your own limits in an attempt to keep up with others. This can lead to burnout, if you push yourself too hard.

In the long-term, competitiveness affects your mental health and your motivation, because being at the top is short-lived, especially within the fast-paced acting industry.

Sooner or later, you will come across one of your peers–or even think of them–who is doing better than you.

At that moment, your serotonin will go down, making you feel depleted.

In this way, serotonin can demotivate you just as easily as it can motivate you.

When you are doing better than others, it is motivating and gives you the fuel to push yourself to ever-greater heights in your career.

On the other hand, facing someone who is

doing better than you lowers your serotonin and puts you in danger of losing your motivation.

SEROTONIN AS A MOTIVATIONAL FUEL

Despite its problems, using serotonin to make progress in your acting career has a distinct advantage over relying on willpower.

When you are fueled by serotonin, you don't need to push yourself. Your brain chemistry does the pushing for you.

The problem is that your level of serotonin depends on how you are doing in relation to others.

As such, serotonin is not a reliable motivation source.

Instead, your motivation is likely to go up and down, instead of being under your own control.

In addition, allowing serotonin to be your primary motivator can cause burnout.

As a result, an over-reliance on serotonin can lead to problems for your physical and mental health.

Fortunately, there is another happy chemical–dopamine–over which you have more control, and which can act as a natural fuel in the same way as serotonin.

We will explore how to work with dopamine in the next chapter.

- A big mistake actors make is to focus their attention on doing better than their peers.
- Competitiveness encourages your brain to release serotonin, a "happy chemical" that is energizing and motivating.
- The problem is that serotonin is an unreliable motivation source, as it stops flowing when you encounter someone doing better than you.
- To regain your higher status, serotonin motivates you to push yourself beyond your limits, which can lead to burnout and to a gradual decline in your mental health.

CHAPTER 4

DOPAMINE AS A MOTIVATIONAL FUEL

A SUSTAINABLE SOURCE OF MOTIVATION

As we discussed in the previous two chapters, neither willpower, nor serotonin, are sustainable sources of motivation. In fact, they can both become demotivating.

If you rely too much on your willpower, there is not enough external pressure to make your efforts sustainable.

Willpower is a finite resource, so it is not a good source of "fuel" for your motivation.

Once your willpower runs out, and the short-lived "honeymoon phase" of taking on a new goal comes to an end, you are likely to feel demotivated and depleted.

Serotonin can work as a fuel, at least for a while. Using competitiveness with your fellow actors as a motivating force does improve your work ethic and ability to get things done.

However, constantly comparing yourself with others is not good for your mental or physical health, nor for your relationships with your fellow actors.

While trying to maintain your position in an industry that is continuously shifting, you end up running yourself into the ground.

As such, it is only a matter of time before relying too much on serotonin becomes demotivating as well.

To keep up your momentum without depleting yourself, you need a sustainable source of motivation.

Dopamine provides the ideal solution and can increase your intrinsic motivation over time.

DOPAMINE AND EVOLUTION

Dopamine is a happy chemical–like serotonin, but different in function–that your brain releases when you set your sights on a goal and start pursuing it.

This natural mood booster is your brain's way

of motivating you to look for potential rewards in your environment and start pursuing them.

It is because of dopamine that you get the initial "honeymoon phase" when you set a new goal or begin working on a new project.

The reason dopamine is such an excellent source of intrinsic motivation is its evolutionary history.

Dopamine motivated our ancestors to search for potential rewards–such as sources of food–and gave them the energy to pursue those rewards.

As such, from an evolutionary perspective, dopamine is ideally suited to be the primary source of fuel for your motivation.

THE BENEFITS OF DOPAMINE

Unlike serotonin, dopamine does not depend on how others are doing.

Dopamine does not go down as a result of changes in your external circumstances and the success of those around you.

This makes dopamine especially useful as a motivating fuel within the acting industry, where it is easy to get distracted from your own goals by focusing too much on your competition.

If dopamine is your primary source of motivation, you will find it easier to maintain your focus long-term.

When fueled by dopamine, you also don't need much willpower, as setting and pursuing goals is energizing and motivating. This creates a positive feedback loop.

The more you get into the habit of setting the right goals, pursuing them, and achieving them, the more energized and motivated you become to reach even bigger goals, creating an exhilarating sense of momentum.

You can use dopamine for the productivity-related aspects of your acting career as well as for keeping up your enthusiasm while doing the boring jobs you are likely to get at the start.

You are already using dopamine in your daily life without realizing it.

For example, if you are in the habit of playing video games, it is because of dopamine that you experience the joy of reaching your goals and develop the motivation to continue playing.

However, if you are not using dopamine intentionally, you are probably not making full use of its benefits.

In the next chapter, we will explore how to

encourage your brain to release dopamine when working on your acting career.

KEY POINTS

- The most sustainable way to increase your motivation is dopamine, a "happy chemical" your brain releases when you set a goal and start pursuing it.
- Unlike serotonin, your level of dopamine does not depend on how anyone else is doing. This makes it a great way to increase your intrinsic motivation without getting distracted.
- Once you are fueled by dopamine, you also don't need much willpower, as dopamine makes you excited to pursue your goals.

.

CHAPTER 5

DOPAMINE HACKS

BRAIN CHEMISTRY AND CONSCIOUS INTENT

Your brain releases dopamine in response to specific external factors.

To identify these factors, it helps to understand the evolutionary principles that govern dopamine release.

Unless you pay close attention to fluctuations in your motivation, dopamine gets released without your conscious intent.

You probably enjoyed the burst of motivation in the past without working out the exact elements that brought it about.

As we start discussing these evolutionary principles, you may recognize them from your own experience.

By actively thinking about these principles in your daily life, you can exert control over your brain chemistry, which will increase your intrinsic motivation.

This will allow you to build an unstoppable sense of momentum with your acting career, instead of leaving your motivation at the mercy of random events.

PRINCIPLES OF DOPAMINE RELEASE

Setting a goal

Your brain releases dopamine when you set a goal and start pursuing it.

It is important to realize that the mere act of setting a goal encourages your brain to release dopamine.

This can work to your advantage, but it can also lead to problems–see the discussion on "shiny new idea syndrome" in the next chapter.

At a deep level, we equate pursuing a goal with meeting our survival needs, which is why setting a new goal is so effective as a motivation booster.

Our brain craves goals. They are the modern

equivalent of the food sources our ancestors were continuously looking for in their environment.

Those of our ancestors who made the most effort in pursuing goals were able to secure more food and better living conditions, which gave them better chances to pass on their genes.

This goal-seeking behavior has profoundly influenced our brain.

As we are the descendants of those who were more goal-focused than their contemporaries, our brain has evolved in a way that favors such behavior.

When you set a goal, your ancient brain thinks, "There's a juicy reward–let's go after it!" and releases a burst of dopamine to give you the energy you need.

Deciding on a "finish line"

Having a clear "finish line" is essential to maximizing the amount of dopamine your brain releases when you set a new goal.

You may think that all goals have a "finish line," but that is not the case.

For example, a learning goal does not have a clear finish line.

If you were to start learning a particular accent, at what point would you declare that goal complete?

With goals that do not have an end in themselves, you therefore have to decide on your own definition of a "finish line."

It is this "finish line" that encourages your brain to release dopamine, both at the beginning, as you start pursuing the new goal, and as you reach various milestones along the way.

Our ancestors, continuously looking for food, did not have vague goals, such as "get better at running."

With the kinds of rewards they pursued, it was clear whether they had reached their goal or not, for example, "Found enough food to survive another day."

When you set a "finish line," your brain will reward this clarity of purpose by releasing more dopamine.

Clarifying the path to the goal

To make the goal you set even more motivating, make sure you are clear on how you will reach it.

Do you know exactly what to do to reach the finish line you set for yourself?

The fewer obstructions are in your way, and the more clarity you have about how to overcome them, the more dopamine your brain will release.

For our ancestors, a clear path to their goal–usually food–meant their reward was within sight.

They could see the lion they were hunting; all they had to work out was how to kill the lion before the lion had a chance to kill them.

No matter how hungry or tired our ancestors were, seeing a clear path to the goal gave them the energy to keep going long enough to reach that all-important food source.

Reaching their goal meant they would eat and get to live another day.

As our brain is shaped by this evolutionary requirement to find a clear path to the goal, you can encourage your brain to release dopamine by deciding on a specific strategy.

A goal such as, "Contact potential agents," is too vague to be effective.

Instead, you need to figure out how you will pursue your goal.

Are you going to write to potential agents?

Attend relevant networking events and introduce yourself? Invite them to see a play you are in?

Decide on the strategy you will use to reach your goal and stick to it for as long as it works.

Identifying your milestones

Milestones are like mini-goals that lead to small bursts of dopamine, increasing your motivation as you advance towards the finish line.

What milestones can you envisage reaching along the way?

Each milestone encourages your brain to release another spurt of dopamine.

This is why so many people swear by to-do lists and love ticking off tasks on these lists.

A whole industry of planners and similar stationery has evolved because of this love we have, as humans, to see ourselves reach the milestones we set.

In chapter 11, you will learn a tool that makes this love of lists and milestones even more effective than the classic "to-do list" you may have used in the past.

Setting ambitious goals

The more ambitious the goal you set, the more dopamine your brain will release.

For our ancestors, "ambitious" usually meant more food and better living conditions, which translated to better chances of survival. No wonder our brain likes big goals.

Pursuing a big goal, such as hunting down a large animal, provided our ancestors with more security for the future than going after small goals, such as looking for a few berries, that would only last enough for one meal.

However, this evolutionary craving for ambitious goals does not mean setting such goals is to be recommended, especially for actors.

The kind of ambitious goals that are relevant for you will likely take a long time to come to fruition.

Such goals come with a high risk of failure, leaving you depleted before you reach the end.

Although an ambitious goal will initially lead to a bigger dopamine release, you can complete achievable goals quicker, and with less risk.

When you set lots of small and achievable goals, you gain access to more dopamine–and therefore motivation–over the long term than if you set one ambitious goal that takes a lot of time and effort to achieve.

For a more in-depth discussion on this topic, see chapter 7.

Setting a new goal

Since setting a goal encourages your brain to release dopamine, a new goal is more motivating than a goal you have been working towards for some time.

Our ancestors did not pursue long-term goals. The kinds of rewards they went after had to be reached quickly, within hours or days, rather than weeks, months, or years.

As such, once you have been pursuing a goal for a while, and the novelty aspect–which generates dopamine–has worn off, your brain starts looking for a new target in the hope of a quicker win.

This might sound like it would be a good idea to switch goals all the time. Of course, this is not the case. Do not abandon your current goal in favor of a new one.

Unless your new goal can be completed at lightning speed, you will soon encounter the same difficulties when an even newer goal appears–a classic case of "shiny new idea syndrome," which we will discuss in the next chapter.

Instead, you may want to consider setting lots of milestones on the path to your goal. To your brain, these will appear like mini-goals.

As you will reach each milestone quickly, the small boosts in dopamine along the way will help you stay motivated despite the long-term nature of your goal.

Quick-to-reach goals

Goals that are quick to reach generate more dopamine than goals that take a long time.

This makes sense from an evolutionary perspective.

Our ancestors were hungry, looking for food. If they saw a food source that was quick to reach, their brain released extra dopamine to allow them to access it.

By contrast, something that would take a long time to reach would not lead to as much dopamine; they would be more likely to keep scanning their environment for easier rewards.

However, in today's world, the problem is that

if you go with this evolutionary principle of prioritizing quick-to-reach over far-off goals, you end up with superficial achievements that fizzle out quickly.

Long-term goals are necessary in today's world, especially for actors.

Your path to any meaningful progress in your career is likely to take many years.

However, there is a way to satisfy this evolutionary need for a quick-to-reach goal: set lots of easily reachable milestones.

By doing so, you are encouraging your brain to release dopamine consistently, while also making it possible to pursue long-term goals to advance your career.

A PROCESS YOU CAN TRUST

Becoming aware of the principles that govern dopamine release means that you now have a set of rules you can follow that are guaranteed to increase your motivation.

Instead of doubting yourself at every turn, you will be able to bring focus to your actions.

As these principles are based on how our brain

has evolved, you can trust that by following them, your intrinsic motivation will grow.

In addition to understanding the principles that govern dopamine release, you must also become aware of certain problems associated with dopamine's addictive quality.

We will explore these potential problems, and how to avoid them, in the next chapter.

KEY POINTS

- Your brain releases dopamine in response to external factors, based on evolutionary principles.
- The mere act of setting a goal stimulates dopamine.
- Your brain also releases dopamine when that goal has a defined end-point, with plenty of milestones along the way and a clear path to the "finish line."
- The more you learn how to adhere to these principles when setting goals, the easier it becomes to motivate yourself while working on your acting career.

CHAPTER 6

DOPAMINE AS ADDICTIVE

PROBLEMS ASSOCIATED WITH DOPAMINE

Despite all the incredible benefits dopamine brings as a motivational fuel, it also comes with a serious problem: just like serotonin, it is addictive.

Dopamine and serotonin are called "happy chemicals" because they boost your mood.

It makes sense that when we experience an increase in such amazing natural mood-boosters, we crave more.

These mood-boosters served the evolutionary purpose of increasing our chances of survival as a species.

As a result, your brain interprets any attempts

to increase your dopamine level as a positive step to ensuring your survival.

The problem is that in our modern world, where you don't have to hunt or forage for food to survive, it is easy to encourage your brain to release dopamine, but not in a way that is healthy for your body or mind.

In this chapter, we will explore two negative consequences dopamine addiction can have on your acting career: "shiny new idea syndrome" and workaholism.

Keeping these potential problems at the back of your mind will allow you to benefit from the motivating power of dopamine, while avoiding its pitfalls.

SHINY NEW IDEA SYNDROME

"Shiny new idea syndrome" refers to shifting your focus towards a new goal when running into difficulties pursuing your current goal.

Because dopamine is so addictive, and setting a new goal releases dopamine, there is a danger of falling into this trap.

For example, you may initially set the goal of putting on a show with your friends.

However, once the novelty wears off and doing the work starts to feel difficult, your attention might shift to some other goal.

You may decide to put together a showreel, and then when that gets too much, you might start working on a new accent, or learning to play the piano.

You could carry on like this for months or years, jumping from one goal to the next, without reaching any of your goals.

When you allow yourself to get lured by the prospect of an easy dopamine fix instead of working on your current goal, you have difficulty bringing anything to fruition.

This becomes demotivating long-term, because you get the biggest boost in dopamine when you reach your goal.

If you consistently give up on your goals, you are likely to lose confidence in your ability to get anything done.

You will get less motivated with every goal you set, because deep down, you will doubt whether you can achieve it.

We often think of unsuccessful people as not doing enough. But often, the problem is the reverse.

The reason someone may be unsuccessful is that they take on too many goals, yet bring none of them to fruition.

To overcome this problem and avoid falling into shiny new idea syndrome, remember that the simple act of setting a goal stimulates dopamine and can become addictive.

Get into the habit of recognizing when you are in danger of being lured away from your current goal by shiny new idea syndrome.

Learning to identify shiny new idea syndrome when the temptation arises will make it easier to remain focused on your current goal.

WORKAHOLISM

The other common problem associated with the addictiveness of dopamine is workaholism.

You may become so obsessed with your acting goals that you neglect every other aspect of your life.

Initially, given you would like to make progress with your acting career, becoming a workaholic may not sound too bad.

After all, if you are going to get addicted to anything, you may as well get addicted to something you want to accomplish–working on your acting career–instead of alcohol, drugs, or anything of that nature.

While this may sound like a good problem to have, getting "high" on dopamine through becoming a workaholic comes with its own set of problems.

If you overdo things because of the addictive nature of dopamine, you will get burned out, which will affect your motivation.

You may also become so obsessed with your goals that you end up distancing yourself from your friends and family.

This may hinder your efforts, because to succeed as an actor, you need a strong support network of people who can pick you up when you are down.

To avoid falling into workaholism, use your willpower to set boundaries not just for working, but also for taking time off to relax and recharge.

Although taking regular breaks may seem like you are slowing down, you are in fact speeding up.

The benefits you get from feeling refreshed will allow you to make quicker progress and give you time to nurture other important areas of your life.

A GOOD EXTERNAL FRAMEWORK

To overcome the potential problems associated with dopamine addiction, you need to use tools that will steer your dopamine flow in the right direction.

The great thing about dopamine is that it is self-sustaining.

But like the water in a river, it needs an external framework to keep it together and make it flow in the right direction.

You can avoid the problems associated with the addictiveness of dopamine if you set up structures and use tools that guide your behavior, instead of allowing the addictiveness of dopamine to affect your good intentions.

In the next few chapters, we will explore a set of simple yet effective tools that can help you avoid distractions, while also making space in your life for rest and relaxation.

We will start with the most basic of these tools, which is about learning how to set goals for your acting career that are achievable and motivating.

- One major problem with dopamine is that it is addictive.
- "Shiny new idea syndrome," the tendency to shift your focus towards a new goal when encountering difficulties with the current one, can lead to not bringing any of your projects to fruition.
- The addictiveness of dopamine can also lead to workaholism. If you start overdoing things because of the addictive nature of dopamine, you will get burned out and isolated.
- You can avoid these problems if you set up structures to guide your behavior, instead of being at the mercy of your dopamine cravings.

CHAPTER 7

GOAL-SETTING FOR ACTORS

ACHIEVABLE VS. AMBITIOUS GOALS

Why dedicate a whole chapter to setting achievable goals? Is that not simply common sense?

In fact, there is much to discuss.

As briefly mentioned in chapter 5, here is the dilemma: ambitious goals are more motivating than achievable goals in the initial stages, so they represent a temptation.

When you set your sights on an ambitious goal, your brain releases more dopamine than when you set an achievable one, because an ambitious goal is more appealing.

From an evolutionary perspective, a big reward—hunting a lion—was better for our ancestors than a small reward; reaching an ambitious goal gave them better chances of survival.

The problem with setting an ambitious goal in our modern-day world, where such goals take a long time to reach, is that doing so requires enormous willpower and considerable energy reserves.

Such goals work if you can sprint towards the finish line and then take time to recover, but that is not the case with most of the goals that are relevant to actors.

Building momentum in your acting career takes time, so you need to adopt a marathon rather than a sprint mindset with most of the goals you set.

As discussed in a previous chapter, willpower is a limited resource that is not easily replenished without a lot of rest.

When you set an ambitious goal, you often run out of willpower quickly and do not have the energy to keep going.

This means you may be tempted to give up on your goal halfway through completion.

By contrast, achievable goals work differently. You only need a small amount of willpower to accomplish an achievable goal, and can therefore maintain consistency.

This long-term sustainability makes achievable goals ideal for your purposes as an actor.

HOW TO SET AN ACHIEVABLE GOAL

Setting an achievable goal is simple: you break whatever task you are working on into the smallest possible steps.

You then turn the first of these steps into your initial goal.

You can set achievable goals while working on a large project, such as putting on a play.

In such cases, the achievable goal may look like a task list, such as, "decide on play," "find suitable location," and so on.

You can also set achievable goals to establish certain habits, such as starting a regular gym routine.

In such cases, the achievable goal may be about what you are planning to do as a minimum every day towards that new habit.

HOW ACHIEVABLE GOALS INCREASE MOTIVATION

Although your brain will only release a small amount of dopamine when you set an achievable goal, you reach it quickly.

When you do, you get a larger dopamine boost for completing your goal.

This gives you the energy and motivation to go after another achievable goal, one that is perhaps slightly more ambitious.

Because of the previous boost in energy, that second goal is also well within reach.

This sets in motion a positive feedback cycle that speeds up your progress and gives rise to a feeling of exhilarating momentum.

In the long term, achievable goals allow you to make progress on your acting career faster than ambitious goals.

Achievable goals also help you build a history of success, which boosts your self-confidence.

As you reach one goal after another, your brain gradually gets the message that you are on a winning streak and provides added dopamine to keep going. Success breeds success.

Your speed increases, and you build momentum. This comes with motivation, extra energy, and all the other benefits of dopamine.

Over time, you become an unstoppable force to be reckoned with.

TIPS FOR SETTING ACHIEVABLE GOALS

Do not be tempted into setting too many goals at once, even achievable ones.

Working on one or two goals a day for your acting career is enough.

If you work on one or two goals consistently, it is amazing how much you can accomplish in a week or a month.

Although, as a rule of thumb, it is best to set achievable goals, it is worth knowing that ambitious goals are appropriate to use in certain circum-stances.

For example, if you are writing a screenplay, and you find yourself going on too many tangents with your story, you may want to set yourself an ambitious deadline, such as finishing the draft in three days.

You may not complete the screenplay by your deadline, but you will get further ahead with your project than if you had set an achievable goal.

The key in this scenario is that, after the three days are done, you can take time to rest and recover. In this way, you are preventing burnout.

Only use ambitious goals in a "sprint" situation, if there is an end-point that is defined and quick to reach.

In the next chapter, we will discuss how to set an achievable daily time goal that will help you fit your acting-related work into the rest of your day.

KEY POINTS

- Both achievable and ambitious goals are motivating, but only achievable goals lead to the consistency you need to generate momentum in your acting career.
- When you set achievable goals and you reach them one after the other, your motivation goes up.
- By contrast, ambitious goals require so much willpower that they become demotivating if you fail to reach them.
- Only set ambitious goals if you can race to the finish line and take plenty of time to recover.

CHAPTER 8

SETTING A TIME GOAL

HOW TO SET A TIME GOAL

Working on your acting career requires making time for it while juggling bill-paying jobs, self-care, your social life, and many other commitments.

In this chapter, we will explore setting a daily time goal.

This will make it possible to fit any work you must do for your acting career into the rest of your day, despite all your other commitments.

A time goal won't work for all your acting-related activities.

For example, it may not work for the time you spend going to auditions, as you do not have control over how long you will wait to be seen.

However, there are many acting-related tasks for which this tool is perfect, such as learning lines, working on your showreel, or practicing a new accent.

This tool will help you find time in your day to work on your acting career.

It will also allow you to relax and recharge guilt-free, once you complete your time goal.

The mechanics of setting a time goal are simple: at the start of your day, set a timer for how long you will work on acting-related tasks before the day is over.

You could set the timer for half an hour, one hour, or two hours–however long you are confident you will be able to spend on your acting career.

The idea is not to accomplish this time goal in one sitting, but rather to divide this total time goal into shorter sprints–see the next chapter–and keep working towards this goal over the course of your day.

The amount of time you aim for is less important than your ability to reach this goal by the end of the day.

Whenever you do something towards your acting career, even the odd five or ten minutes, let the timer run.

By the end of the day, make sure you complete the time you have decided on.

HOW SETTING A TIME GOAL INCREASES MOTIVATION

A time goal gives you a clear "finish line" to work towards.

This is motivating, as it encourages your brain to release dopamine the closer the timer gets to zero.

The timer allows you flexibility over when you work towards your acting goals, while also keeping you accountable to yourself.

Setting a time goal makes it easier to integrate your acting-related work into the rest of your day, even if you must juggle lots of other commitments.

By setting boundaries around the time you spend on your acting career, you will also be able to eliminate any guilt that might come up when you use your spare time to relax and recharge.

The timer gives you a clear standard by which you can measure whether you have done enough for your acting career on any given day.

You can then devote any remaining time to relaxing and replenishing your energy.

In this way, you can make great strides in your acting career and also avoid slipping into workaholism.

TIPS FOR SETTING A TIME GOAL

Consistency is more important than how much time you set as your goal.

It is amazing how much you can get done in thirty minutes each day, if you use that time well– the next chapter will help you do that.

An ideal time goal might be one hour a day, if that is feasible, given your other commitments.

Imagine how much you could get done towards your acting career if you dedicated one hour every day to it.

Even if more time opens up in your schedule, don't suddenly increase the size of your goal; build up the time gradually.

If you jump from one hour to three hours, you are setting yourself up for failure.

You may be able to do it for a few days, but there will come a day when you won't have the energy to complete your overly ambitious goal.

You are likely to experience this as a failure, which will demotivate you, when the actual problem is that you set too ambitious a goal to remain consistent.

You may, however, occasionally have to adjust your time goal downwards to fit in with your circumstances.

For example, if you have an important deadline at your bill-paying job on a particular day, you may only have ten minutes available to dedicate to your acting career.

If so, it is best to aim for a more modest time goal that day, instead of attempting to reach your usual goal and falling short.

It is also a good idea to decide in advance that you will not work on your acting career on a particular day, if you know that you cannot fit in the time.

Otherwise, if you decide to do a certain amount of time on your acting career and you don't, your mind will see it as a failure.

This will make it more difficult to motivate yourself the following day.

Remember to prioritize achievability over ambition.

It is better to be realistic about what you can do within your given circumstances, instead of aiming high and then feeling disappointed you didn't reach your goal.

If you don't reach your goal one day, don't try to make up for it the following day. Do your best and forget the rest.

Sometimes, life gets in the way, even when you set an achievable time goal.

However, make sure that failing to reach your daily time goal does not become a regular thing.

If you miss more than two days in a row, maybe you need to lower your time goal.

Once you reach your goal, it is best to stop for the day, even if you have time to do more work.

The timer going down to zero is when you get your maximum dopamine boost, which motivates you to work towards your goal again the next day.

Do not change the goalpost and deprive yourself of that big reward.

Use any available time after you reached your goal to relax and recharge, instead of filling it with more acting-related tasks. You worked hard and deserve a break.

In the next chapter, we will explore how to divide up the time you set as your daily time goal into shorter sprints, to maximize your productivity and build a delightful sense of momentum.

- At the start of your day, set a goal for the total amount of time you will work on your acting career before the day is over, and set a timer to track your progress.

- As the timer gets closer to zero, you will get more dopamine, which will motivate you to keep going.

- This tool allows you to make space in your day for your acting-related work, while also giving you guilt-free time to relax and recharge.

- Be realistic when setting your goal and prioritize consistency over ambition.

CHAPTER 9

WORK SPRINTS

HOW TO USE WORK SPRINTS

In the previous chapter, we explored how to set a time goal to fit your acting-related work into your day in a way that is motivating and sustainable.

In this chapter, we will discuss how to use this time.

Specifically, we will explore work sprints as a tool to increase both your productivity and motivation while working on your acting career.

To do a work sprint, choose a career-related task to work on–for example, updating your acting CV–and set your timer for a short amount of time, such as five, ten, or fifteen minutes.

You should set one timer for your daily time

goal–see the previous chapter–and another timer for these work sprints.

As soon as the timer starts, work exclusively on your task, with no interruptions, and stop the moment the timer gets to zero; this is your sprint.

Then take a short break, which you can also set a timer for, and repeat the process.

Work sprints are great for tasks such as doing admin work on projects you initiate, undertaking the necessary research into a potential project, or learning your lines.

It is amazing how much progress you can make by using this tool, even if you only have a short amount of time available.

Try using work sprints in conjunction with setting a daily time goal every day for a month.

You will make lots of progress and feel motivated to keep going.

HOW WORK SPRINTS INCREASE MOTIVATION

Working in short bursts keeps your mind focused, more so than if you did not set a defined time limit.

Each sprint gives you an easy-to-reach goal. This is why this tool is so effective as a productivity hack–it stimulates dopamine.

When you combine using short work sprints with setting a daily time goal, each sprint also becomes a milestone on the path to reaching your overall daily goal.

Using work sprints allows you to increase your productivity and make quick progress, even if the task itself is boring.

Using sprints is the easiest way to motivate yourself to complete the boring but necessary tasks that advance your acting career the most–updating your CV, contacting potential agents, or editing your showreel.

These sprints encourage you to do as much as possible during the time you have; they are a great way to avoid procrastination.

TIPS FOR USING WORK SPRINTS

If you experience resistance working on a task, use a five-minute sprint.

Once you overcome your initial resistance by working on the task for five minutes, it becomes easier to build momentum and work on it for longer periods.

Experiment to see what length of time suits you best for your sprints.

You could start with a five-minute sprint to warm up, then increase the length of your sprints to ten or fifteen minutes.

For easy tasks, you can use longer sprints. You do not need as much willpower as you do when working on more difficult tasks.

If you have lost momentum on a task, go back to using shorter sprints to motivate yourself.

In general, shorter sprints are more productive than longer ones.

For example, two twenty-minute sprints will be more productive than a forty-minute sprint, even though the total amount of time is the same.

You are most productive at the end of a sprint, when the finish line is in sight; this is when your brain releases the maximum amount of dopamine.

On the other hand, some tasks require deep focus and may benefit from longer sprints.

Over time, as you keep trying different sprint lengths, you will have a better idea of how long you should sprint for.

Be strict with yourself about stopping once the time is up, even if you would like to continue.

The end-time encourages your brain to release dopamine, so avoid the temptation to change your goalposts.

In addition, due to dopamine, the mind craves completion.

As a result, you will feel motivated to get back to the task during your next sprint to finish what you started.

This means that you will find it easier to get in the zone, which will build momentum and speed up your progress.

Set up breaks in-between your sprints to give yourself time to relax and recharge.

Set a timer for your breaks as well, to avoid losing momentum and drifting into procrastination.

In the next chapter, we will discuss a tool that will allow you to initiate and complete a large-scale project, allowing you to build momentum.

KEY POINTS

- You can structure your daily time goal into short work sprints.
- Working in short bursts gives you an end goal that is easy to reach, which encourages your brain to release dopamine.

- If you experience resistance working on a task, use a five-minute sprint. Once you overcome the initial resistance, it becomes easier to build momentum.
- Be strict with yourself about stopping once the time is up, even if you would like to keep going.
- Make sure to take breaks in-between sprints and set a timer for your breaks as well.

CHAPTER 10

CLOSED LISTS

HOW TO USE CLOSED LISTS

To take your acting career forward, you need to allocate some effort towards being proactive, instead of simply going to auditions and hoping to get cast.

This means you should not rely exclusively on work coming to you, but also develop the skills to initiate your own acting work.

In this chapter, we will discuss how to motivate yourself to complete a large project, such as putting on a play, or making a film with a few of your friends.

Specifically, we will discuss how to use closed

lists to motivate yourself to complete large-scale projects of this kind.

This simple yet powerful tool was put forward by Mark Forster in *Do It Tomorrow* as a way of boosting general productivity and can work wonders for your acting career.

Closed lists are more motivating than the to-do lists many actors use when developing a large-scale project.

What is a closed list?

It is a list of tasks, like a to-do list, but with one important distinction: as the name suggests, a closed list is limited to a specific number of items, ideally no more than ten.

You must complete all the items on your closed list before taking on any new task.

Checklists are a type of closed list you are probably familiar with.

The checklist does not expand beyond the original set of items and you must complete all the items on that list.

However, beyond checklists, you can also create a closed list with a small number of unrelated tasks.

To the untrained eye, a closed list may look similar to a to-do list.

However, it is the mindset shift of not taking on any new tasks before completing the ones already on your list that makes the closed list such a motivating tool for working on large-scale projects.

HOW CLOSED LISTS INCREASE MOTIVATION

A closed list presents several advantages over the usual to-do list.

A to-do list keeps growing, as more tasks come to your attention.

By adding new items to your to-do list, you are changing the goalposts.

The ever-expanding nature of the to-do list makes it demotivating, as your brain only releases dopamine when you have a clear end-point in sight.

The to-do list also comes with another motivational problem.

To keep yourself motivated to work on your ever-expanding to-do list, you end up cherry-picking whatever is easiest and leaving everything else "for later." This usually means it does not get done.

What gets left out is often the most difficult

task, which is also the one that would be the most impactful.

This leads to a backlog and a sense of incompletion.

By contrast, when you use a closed list, every item must get done before you consider taking on any new task.

Even if you do all the easiest tasks on a closed list first, you still get around to doing the more difficult ones, because nothing gets left out on a closed list; that is the cardinal rule of using this tool.

A closed list can help you finish even the most boring or difficult tasks.

When you get to the last item, you are motivated to get it done, no matter how challenging it is, because completing it takes you to your "finish line."

Each task you do represents a milestone that brings you closer to reaching your goal–completing the entire list.

Ticking one item after the other is motivating when there is a clear end in sight.

As a result, you get a dopamine boost every time you finish a task, as you are one step closer to the finish line.

TIPS FOR USING CLOSED LISTS

If a task feels too difficult, break it down into its component parts and turn it into a closed list of smaller tasks.

When you do so, you are making it more motivating to complete the original task.

Put no more than ten tasks on your closed list. The shortness of the list makes it motivating to work on, as your goal of completing the list is within easy reach.

Don't worry about the order in which you tackle the tasks, but make sure you get all of them done before taking on any additional work.

If you must add more tasks, draw a line at the bottom of your closed list and add the new items below the line, to a new closed list.

In this way, the original list remains closed, and the new items are part of a different list you will only tackle once you have cleared your existing list.

As such, these new items will not distract you from working on your current list, nor will adding these items feel demotivating.

In the next chapter, we will explore a tool you can use to increase your motivation when working on repetitive tasks.

These kinds of tasks do not have a clear end-point, so you cannot put them on a closed list.

KEY POINTS

- As an actor, you should not rely exclusively on auditions, but also initiate your own projects.
- When working on large-scale projects, such as putting on a show, many actors make the mistake of using to-do lists rather than closed lists.
- The problem with the to-do list is that it keeps expanding, which is demotivating.
- When your end-goal changes, your brain does not release the dopamine you need to remain consistent. This often leads to abandoning the project instead of bringing it to completion.
- By contrast, ticking one item after the other on a closed list is motivating. Every task you tackle on that list takes you one step closer to your end goal.

CHAPTER 11

GAME-IFYING YOUR PROGRESS

HOW TO GAME-IFY YOUR PROGRESS

In the previous chapter, we discussed how to motivate yourself to complete all the tasks relating to a project by using closed lists.

However, many of the tasks you need motivation for as an actor are not about completing one big project; they are repetitive and–some of them–long-term.

This may include going to auditions, learning lines, or working on your fitness.

The easiest way to encourage your brain to release dopamine in these situations is to game-ify what you are doing by competing with yourself.

For example, let's say you are trying to motivate yourself to go to more auditions.

The most likely outcome of going to an audition is rejection, which is painful to experience over and over.

On the other hand, finding the right opportunity is often a numbers game. As such, going to lots of auditions increases your chances of getting cast.

This means you must motivate yourself to go to lots of auditions, despite the many rejections you are likely to receive.

In this type of situation, game-ifying your progress provides the ideal solution.

As you are likely to get lots of rejections anyway, you may as well turn this into a game.

You can game-ify going to auditions by setting a monthly rejection target.

At the start of the month, set an easily achievable rejection target, based on the average number of rejections you get.

Once you reach your monthly target for three consecutive months, set a slightly higher target for the following month, and aim to reach that consistently for another three months.

Using this process will help you increase the

overall number of auditions you go to, and therefore, improve your chances of success.

By game-ifying the experience of getting lots of rejections, you are setting yourself up for a motivating situation no matter how things turn out.

If you receive a callback, or get the part, your brain will release dopamine and your motivation will increase because you have reached your ultimate goal.

But if you don't hear back, you will still increase your motivation, because you are one step closer to reaching your rejection target and outdoing your previous efforts.

By game-ifying rejections in this way, you are motivating yourself to keep going to auditions with only minimal willpower.

As getting cast is often a numbers game, this strategy will do wonders for both your acting career and your motivation.

HOW GAME-IFYING YOUR PROGRESS INCREASES MOTIVATION

Game-ifying any task you must do repeatedly encourages your brain to release dopamine.

The more dopamine your brain releases in

response to the game-ification aspect, the more motivated you will be to do that task.

As such, you will need less willpower to keep doing the task over and over.

Game-ifying your progress works especially well with tasks that feel difficult and require willpower.

When you game-ify your progress, you are making repetitive or difficult tasks fun.

As you improve upon your previous achievements, the changes in brain chemistry make you excited to see how much further you can push yourself.

Using game-ification, you are also likely to become more creative in how you achieve your goals.

Your process is likely to improve the more you repeat the task.

For example, the more auditions you go to, the better you will get at auditioning.

Unlike competing with others, aiming to beat your own score keeps everything within your control.

This makes game-ifying your progress a sustainable way to keep pushing yourself.

The better you do, the more your results will

improve and the more motivated you will be to keep going.

By game-ifying your progress, you are setting up a positive feedback loop that makes improvement inevitable.

TIPS FOR GAME-IFYING YOUR PROGRESS

To ensure you make game-ifying your progress as motivating as possible, set an initial goal that is easily achievable.

This will eliminate resistance and ensure you do not deplete yourself.

In addition, set each subsequent target only minimally higher than the one before.

This will allow you to reach each of your new targets quickly and benefit from the motivating effects of dopamine.

However, beware of the addictiveness of game-ifying your progress.

The more skilled you get at using this tool, the more addictive the activity you are game-ifying becomes. Beware of going overboard and veering into workaholism.

For example, you can take going to the gym too far, to the point where you spend all your time at the gym and don't have energy for anything else.

If you tend to fall into this trap, it is important to set boundaries for yourself to relax, recharge, and take care of the other areas of your life that require your attention.

KEY POINTS

- For repetitive tasks that require willpower, such as going to auditions, the easiest way to motivate yourself is to game-ify your progress.
- Set an easy target and once you reach it consistently, set a higher goal going forward.
- Game-ifying repetitive tasks puts you in control, as you are not competing with anyone else, and motivates you to keep going, despite not having an end-goal.
- This tool can become addictive, so set healthy boundaries that allow you time to relax, recharge, and take care of the other important aspects of your life.

CHAPTER 12

PRINCIPLES OVER TOOLS

USING CONSCIOUS INTENT

Over the previous five chapters, we have explored a few simple yet powerful tools that will encourage your brain to release dopamine and motivate you to work harder on your acting career.

Using these tools will create external circumstances that make it easy for your intrinsic motivation to grow, one small accomplishment at a time.

In this chapter, we will explore how these tools, and others you will find along the way, help you build momentum in your acting career.

Central to everything you are learning throughout this book is the notion of intentionally changing your brain chemistry.

In doing so, you are making it possible to boost your motivation at will, instead of leaving it at the mercy of your shifting moods.

It is this attitude of actively thinking about your brain chemistry that will create the biggest change in the way you approach working on your acting career.

The more conscious control you develop over your motivation, the more progress you will make, building an exhilarating sense of momentum.

This begins with encouraging your brain to release dopamine.

DOPAMINE AND YOUR FRAMEWORK AS ALLIES

When considering how to increase your motivation, it is not the tools that are the most important; it is the principles underpinning these tools that you need to keep in mind.

As such, when considering your motivation, prioritize principles over tools.

Remember the principles you learned in chapter 5, that govern how your brain releases dopamine.

Set goals for yourself and make sure these goals are achievable.

Decide on your end-point in advance, with plenty of milestones along the way and a clear strategy for reaching the "finish line."

For repetitive tasks that do not have a clear end-point, game-ify your progress to stay motivated.

By keeping these principles of dopamine release at the forefront of your mind, you will create the momentum to take your acting career to the next level.

BUILDING LIFE-LONG SKILLS

When facing a motivation problem, ask yourself what framework you can put in place to encourage your brain to release dopamine.

Do you need to make your goal more easily achievable? Set a daily time goal? Use work sprints? List your tasks using a closed list so you can tick them off one by one? Game-ify your progress?

Get into the habit of asking yourself how to nurture your motivation and use the most effective tools for that purpose.

By using the right tools for whatever motivation problem you have, you can build a powerful framework that will encourage your brain to release dopamine whenever you need a motivation boost.

In the next chapter, we will discuss particular moments in your acting career when you may struggle with your motivation, and how to apply what you have learned to those situations.

KEY POINTS

- Start thinking about how to encourage your brain to release dopamine.
- When facing a motivation barrier, ask yourself what structures and tools you can use to overcome it.
- Understanding the principles of working with your brain chemistry is key to mastering your motivation.

CHAPTER 13

HOW TO TURN BORING
INTO FUN

OVERCOMING BOREDOM

Aside from helping with productivity, dopamine can also motivate you to turn boring into fun.

For example, at the beginning of your acting career, you may have to take on acting jobs that might not be as creative and inspiring as you would like.

Although boring, these jobs provide useful networking opportunities that will make it possible to find better work further down the line.

As such, you need to keep yourself motivated so you can show up to these jobs enthusiastic and energized, the kind of actor people in the industry love to work with and recommend to their colleagues.

When considering how to turn boring into fun, it is worth remembering the principles behind dopamine release.

To keep up your motivation during times of boredom, set a goal for yourself.

This goal can be anything that sounds stimulating or productive, such as learning a new skill, improving your performance on an existing skill, learning lines, and so on.

For example, on one of these boring days you must get through, could you learn to juggle? Or practice a new accent? Or read a good book?

The moment you set a goal of this kind, your brain will start releasing dopamine.

To keep encouraging your brain to release dopamine throughout your boring day(s), make sure the goal has a clear end-point, with plenty of milestones along the way, and that you can see the path to the "finish line."

The more you learn to keep yourself stimulated in this way, the more fun you will be to work with, which may lead to better opportunities in the future.

Let's explore a few situations you are likely to encounter over the course of your acting career which will require you to motivate yourself through the boring days.

What follows is not a comprehensive list.

It is simply a way to get you thinking about how to use your brain's ability to release dopamine to turn boring into fun in a variety of different scenarios.

The role is not creatively stimulating

Landing a role that is not creatively stimulating is a problem that may occur many times, especially in the early years of your acting career.

This could be work on a commercial you are not enthusiastic about, or a tiny two-dimensional part in a forgettable TV show.

You may have taken the work because there wasn't much else available at the time or because you needed to add to your acting CV.

Regardless of the reasons for taking the job, the lack of motivation is still a problem you need to solve.

If you find yourself in this situation, how can you encourage your brain to release some dopamine?

As mentioned earlier in this book, dopamine is extremely pleasurable, hence its addictive qualities.

This means that any dopamine boost when you are in danger of becoming bored and losing your enthusiasm will instantly improve your mood.

To stimulate dopamine flow, ask yourself what you could do while on this uncreative job that would give you a sense of excitement.

Is there something you could learn while on this job? For example, can you learn a new skill? (How does juggling sound?)

Or could you amuse yourself by speaking to everybody in a new accent you've been practicing?

Make your own creative challenges, such as learning and remembering the names of each member of the production crew as well as a funny story about them.

This would be great for networking and finding work further down the line, but also, it would keep your brain engaged and boost your mood.

Alternatively, you could encourage your brain

to release dopamine by completing something you need to do anyway.

For example, you could use the time to learn lines for your next audition or start working on a new monologue.

Finally, think about what this job allows you to do that is more creative and satisfying, yet maybe does not bring in the cash.

For example, perhaps the money you are earning from this boring job is giving you the time and space to undertake a fun project of your own.

Reframing this job as an exchange for your creative time will make it easier to keep yourself motivated.

Dealing with long show-itis

"Long show-itis" refers to being in a long show run and getting to that point where...well, it feels like the show has gone on for too long.

How do you keep yourself motivated during this type of situation?

Every actor has their way of dealing with it, and I'm sure you do.

But in case you are looking for ways to improve

your existing process, ask yourself how to get your brain to release some dopamine.

Most of those things that work when the role is not creatively stimulating apply here as well.

In addition, think of something novel you can introduce, either as part of your day or as part of the show.

For example, instead of doing your usual warm-up, how about putting together a new warm-up routine, to add some novelty?

Alternatively, if this appeals to you, how about adding something with a small degree of risk during the show?

This would introduce some excitement and make it particularly satisfying when it works out.

The boredom will still be there at times, but actively thinking about ways to encourage your brain to release dopamine will help you better manage your motivation.

Dealing with a small part

Having a small part, especially on stage, can bring up similar issues as when the work is not creative enough or when the show goes on for too long.

You may have been happy to be cast, as work is work, but after a while, the smallness of the part may get to you.

One additional danger with a small part, if this is a stage role, is that if your brain is bored, it is likely to make your life more "interesting" by leading you to forget your lines or drop a prop–the kind of humiliating event that can trigger the onset of stage fright.

As such, do not take your boredom lightly and think, "It's just a matter of getting through this."

Find ways to keep your brain engaged and happy, so it does not lead you to self-sabotage. Think of ways to encourage your brain to release dopamine.

To keep your brain stimulated, find something challenging or interesting to do.

This may need to be offstage, as your fellow actors may not appreciate you taking up too much attention during the show.

Learn a new skill or start a side project–anything that keeps your brain engaged and gives you something meaningful to occupy your mind.

You may also want to use your extra creative energy to initiate additional work for yourself, such as setting up a project with friends.

If you do this successfully, you will get better at managing your motivation even in the absence of outside stimulation–a great skill to have.

When play becomes work

It is common for actors to spend years doing a substantial portion of their acting work for free, or only being able to pay a tiny percentage of their bills through their acting work.

As an actor, you probably have a bill-paying job that supports you financially while you try to get your foot in the door on the acting side.

And then, the right opportunity comes along with your acting career and you start being able to pay all the bills through your acting work.

Here is an interesting problem that may happen at this point: now that you can make a living as an actor, is the fun gone?

First of all, if you are finding yourself in this situation, congratulations! It has probably been a long road to get here and it is an amazing achievement.

Secondly, this is a nice problem to have, but it is still a problem, so don't berate yourself for seeing it as such.

Thirdly, rest assured that feeling this way is more common than you might expect.

From a psychological perspective, your previous motivation to work as an actor was probably boosted by so-called "cognitive dissonance."

When two actions are not congruent with one another, people experience psychological stress.

As a result, they feel motivated to change their thoughts in a way that reconciles these two actions.

In your case, perhaps the two actions you had to reconcile in your mind were: 1) the fact that you were bored doing some of the acting work that came your way, and 2) that you were doing this work for free.

To resolve this dilemma, you may have persuaded yourself that the work was more interesting than it was.

Now that you are getting paid for this work, you are seeing it more objectively.

Cognitive dissonance was demonstrated, among others, by a study in which participants were asked to spend an hour doing a tedious task, such as turning pegs a quarter-turn at regular intervals.

Once the participants had completed the task,

some of the participants were asked to speak to another participant.

Unbeknownst to them, this other participant had been hired by the experimenters.

The real participants were asked to persuade the pretend-participant that the tedious task had been interesting.

In one group, participants were paid one dollar, while participants in a second group were paid twenty dollars.

Participants in a third group were not asked to speak with the pretend-participant.

When asked to rate how much they had enjoyed completing the tedious task, the participants who had been paid one dollar rated it more positively than the participants who had been paid twenty dollars.

They also rated the task as more interesting than the participants who had not spoken to the pretend-participant.

The results of this study suggest that the participants who had only been paid one dollar rationalized having told another person the task had been interesting by changing the way they viewed the task.

By contrast, those participants paid twenty dollars did not engage in this rationalization.

They had been motivated by the significantly higher financial incentive and therefore saw the task more objectively.

Now that "play" has become work, you need to consider how to motivate yourself through the boring days in a new way, as your previous source of motivation no longer works.

Fortunately, you already know the solution: look for ways to encourage your brain to release dopamine.

Set goals relating to your acting work and use all the principles and tools you have been learning throughout this book to make your work as exciting and interesting as possible.

The more dopamine you have available as you transition into getting paid good money for your acting work, the less you will miss the motivation provided by cognitive dissonance.

This shift in the source of your motivation may take some time, as you are having to readjust to a different way of thinking about your work.

Do not despair if, for a while, you feel somewhat unmotivated.

Become curious about how your motivation is changing in response to your career progression and allow yourself time to adjust to this new situation.

It may also be worth discussing these issues with a therapist.

This will give you a safe space to explore all the mindset changes you need to make during this new chapter in your career.

INCREASING MOTIVATION VS. IMPLEMENTING CHANGE

In discussing how to turn boring into fun, we have been working on the premise that increasing your motivation is the best course of action.

Indeed, if you want a long-term career as an actor, you must learn to get through the boring days without dampening your spirit or resorting to unhealthy habits.

However, it is worth noting: not every problem can be solved psychologically.

There may be times in your acting career when, instead of boosting your motivation to make your day more exciting, it may be best to consider whether you should get out of that situation altogether.

If you have a persistent feeling that you are trapped in a bad situation–an unfair contract, a toxic work environment, or a bad working relationship with an agent–you may be right.

In such cases, it is change that is needed, rather than extra motivation.

Do not let your ability to motivate yourself out of boredom become a barrier to implementing much-needed change.

Making the change may be hard, which is probably why you haven't made it before now, but it may be the healthiest course of action.

Learn to distinguish between when you need to boost your motivation by turning boring into fun, and when you need to cut your losses and get out.

That in itself is an important skill, and the better you become at making this distinction, the more your chances of success will increase.

CONCLUSION

As you begin using the tools you have learned in this book to increase your motivation, it is important to give yourself time and patience.

Increasing your motivation requires your brain to start working differently than at present, which in turn requires practice.

The more you practice, the more you give your brain a chance to learn new ways of working.

In addition, practice will teach you how to get yourself out of a rut when you fall into one.

You will soon gain the confidence to increase your motivation yourself, rather than waiting for outside circumstances to change before you feel motivated.

Even so, there will be times, especially at the

beginning, when you will fall back into your old habits and forget to encourage your brain to release dopamine.

You may not notice this until you feel depleted of energy and motivation.

If this happens, do not beat yourself up. Simply use the tools in this book to get yourself energized and motivated once again.

Boosting your motivation and becoming skilled at working with your brain is about trial and error, and getting better over time.

The fact that you have read this book to the end and are taking proactive measures to increase your motivation is already a big step in the right direction.

The progress you will achieve through applying everything you have learned in this book is well worth the effort.

If you can master your motivation, especially without outside validation, you will have a long and successful acting career, and a happy life.

Increasing your motivation is a life skill.

As you learn to use these tools in the context of your acting career, you will also start applying them to other parts of your life.

These skills will not just make your acting

career better–they will improve your life as a whole.

Remember that you are unique, so use the tools in this book as a starting point for developing your own process.

Finally, please consider passing on this knowledge to any actor friends who may need to boost their motivation.

I wish you all the best with your acting career.

I would like to ask you for a small favor.

Reviews are the best way to spread the word about this book. If you have found this book helpful, it would mean a lot to me if you could leave a review.

Even if you write only a sentence or two, it will help. Thank you!

A USEFUL RESOURCE

If you want to improve your chances of success as an actor, psychology can help.

Psychology Tools for Actors teaches you ten simple yet powerful psychology tools to take your acting career to the next level.

Download for free when you sign up for the *Psychology for Actors* newsletter at:

www.psychologyforactors.com/newsletter

ABOUT THE AUTHOR

Alexa Ispas holds a PhD in psychology from the University of Edinburgh.

The books in her *Psychology for Actors Series* provide actors with proven psychology techniques to thrive and build a successful career.

If you'd like to stay in touch with Alexa and learn more psychological tools that are directly relevant to actors, please sign up for the *Psychology for Actors* newsletter. You will receive a short free book when you sign up.

You can sign up for the newsletter and receive your free book at:

www.psychologyforactors.com/newsletter

Memorization for Actors

Self-Confidence for Actors

Resilience for Actors

Motivation for Actors

Excellence for Actors

Success for Actors

For more information, please visit:

www.psychologyforactors.com

Printed in Great Britain
by Amazon

22959771R00065